Follow me on Instagram for daily posts!

 NoraReidColoring

Copyright © 2021 Nora Reid

All rights reserved. No part of this publication may be reproduced, distributed or transmitted in any form or by any means, including photocopying, recording, or other electronic or mechanical methods, without the prior written permission of the publisher, except in the case of brief quotations embodied in critical reviews and certain other non-commercial uses permitted by copyright law.

Trademarked names appear throughout this book. Rather than use a trademark symbol with every occurrence of a trademarked name, names are used in an editorial fashion, with no intention of infringement of the respective owner's trademark. The information in this book is distributed on an "as is" basis, without warranty. Although every precaution has been taken in the preparation of this work, neither the author nor the publisher shall have any liability to any person or entity with respect to any loss or damage caused or alleged to be caused directly or indirectly by the information contained in this book.

About The Author

Nora Reid is a fun-loving gal who loves letting her hair down, smoking, and relishing the humor of life. She spends her days and nights lost in the blissful world of imagination and the realm of psychedelic art. Nora has a carefree soul and cheery spirit who relishes living in a blissful world of trance and ecstasy. She believes in living life to the fullest, enjoying every moment, and letting her witty sense of humor run wild.

Her mission is to help others in stressful or otherwise upsetting states to release their anger and bring out the best in them, their inner-artist. Everyone has an inner-artist inside them, and these books will be the key to bringing it out. Feel free to check out her other titles by searching for them on Amazon!

If you enjoy this book please consider leaving a review, it really helps out small publishers like me! For easy access you can scan the QR code below which will take you straight to the review page on Amazon. Thank you in advance! ❤

Table of Contents

Calligraphy 1

Journal 3

Word Searches 11

Mazes 16

Sudoku 26

Stoner Questions 30

Story Time 32

Spot the Difference 33

Stoner Thoughts 37

Joint vs. Spliff vs. Blunt 39

Sativa vs. Indica 40

18 Ways to Get High 41

Best Movies to Watch Stoned 42

Mount Kushmore 43

Weed Around the World 44

Weed Brownie Recipe 45

Weed Facts 47

Coloring In 49

Calligraphy

ABCDEFGHIJKLMN

OPQRSTUVWXYZ

abcdefghijklmn opqrst

uvwxyz 1234567890

Sweet Mary Jane

Aa

Calligraphy

How high am I?

- ○ Nothin' yet...
- ○ I felt something
- ○ You feel something?
- ○ Gettin' there
- ○ Here it comes
- ○ Let's get snacks
- ○ Did you say something?
- ○ What was I saying?
- ○ Woah
- ○ I'm cooked

What am I feeling? _____
_____
_____

What am I doing? _____
_____
_____

What am I thinking? _____
_____
_____

Doodles

Location: _____ Date: _____ Time: _____

How high am I?

- ○ Nothin' yet...
- ○ I felt something
- ○ You feel something?
- ○ Gettin' there
- ○ Here it comes
- ○ Let's get snacks
- ○ Did you say something?
- ○ What was I saying?
- ○ Woah
- ○ I'm cooked

What am I feeling? _____
_____
_____

What am I doing? _____
_____
_____

What am I thinking? _____
_____
_____

Doodles

Location: Date: Time:

How high am I?

- ○ Nothin' yet...
- ○ I felt something
- ○ You feel something?
- ○ Gettin' there
- ○ Here it comes
- ○ Let's get snacks
- ○ Did you say something?
- ○ What was I saying?
- ○ Woah
- ○ I'm cooked

What am I feeling? _____
_____
_____

What am I doing? _____
_____
_____

What am I thinking? _____
_____
_____

Doodles

Location: _____ Date: _____ Time: _____

How high am I?

- ◯ Nothin' yet...
- ◯ I felt something
- ◯ You feel something?
- ◯ Gettin' there
- ◯ Here it comes
- ◯ Let's get snacks
- ◯ Did you say something?
- ◯ What was I saying?
- ◯ Woah
- ◯ I'm cooked

What am I feeling? _____
_____
_____

What am I doing? _____
_____
_____

What am I thinking? _____
_____
_____

Doodles

Location: Date: Time:

How high am I?

- ◯ Nothin' yet...
- ◯ I felt something
- ◯ You feel something?
- ◯ Gettin' there
- ◯ Here it comes
- ◯ Let's get snacks
- ◯ Did you say something?
- ◯ What was I saying?
- ◯ Woah
- ◯ I'm cooked

What am I feeling? _____
_____
_____

What am I doing? _____
_____
_____

What am I thinking? _____
_____
_____

Doodles

Location: Date: Time:

How high am I?

- ◯ Nothin' yet...
- ◯ I felt something
- ◯ You feel something?
- ◯ Gettin' there
- ◯ Here it comes
- ◯ Let's get snacks
- ◯ Did you say something?
- ◯ What was I saying?
- ◯ Woah
- ◯ I'm cooked

What am I feeling? _____
_____
_____

What am I doing? _____
_____
_____

What am I thinking? _____
_____
_____

Doodles

Location: Date: Time:

How high am I?

- ○ Nothin' yet...
- ○ I felt something
- ○ You feel something?
- ○ Gettin' there
- ○ Here it comes
- ○ Let's get snacks
- ○ Did you say something?
- ○ What was I saying?
- ○ Woah
- ○ I'm cooked

What am I feeling? _____
_____
_____

What am I doing? _____
_____
_____

What am I thinking? _____
_____
_____

Doodles

Location: _____ Date: _____ Time: _____

How high am I?

- ○ Nothin' yet...
- ○ I felt something
- ○ You feel something?
- ○ Gettin' there
- ○ Here it comes
- ○ Let's get snacks
- ○ Did you say something?
- ○ What was I saying?
- ○ Woah
- ○ I'm cooked

What am I feeling? _____
_____
_____

What am I doing? _____
_____
_____

What am I thinking? _____
_____
_____

Doodles

Location:					Date:			Time:

Word Search 1

```
U L F N I H K C J I K B M W C
R H R L R V B F M T P P P Y C
J E D G L D H M G E J D H R T
H R R O S D W S T N U L B I D
M B L R C Y U G O E L R I H H
U H M O C N J R B A P G D O J
F E Y A D H P E O M P A T P L
O S G S E O V E N T T B V F M
O U P R P D E N G D O T A N V
E H D E I D I Y L X M H R D P
C E J T F U B B R K D F U V O
N O K R J H U A L A C C E K L
U E M A T H G I E E P H J L A
O R A U M K N A K A S T L O U
V P O Q W N T Y B Y K V L T W
```

BONG   HERB   EIGHT
GREEN   BLUNTS   QUARTERS
THC   HOTBOX   EDIBLES
VAPE   CBD   OUNCE

Word Search 2

```
J Q R F H R F D E K O O C O Y
E A R Q R V A S S Y Y O H P T
T N P U R P L E H A Z E E W S
W R E C K E D J M E S B Y R B
P O U N D D J B A B T O S B P
C A N N A B I N O I D W J G L
M D T J E N W C R W E L B D C
A N I A G R V W X U M B C O V
E K H G I G O P B R I B P O K
R S C O L L E E A S E O B B M
D Y A V J F T E K A A F I I J
E M O L M H E N X L G E E E K
U N R U C N H Q C I L K M E G
L H L I O L P W V T J O H L R
B Q S C U N C J I S K T A N N
```

CONE	REEFER	WRECKED
COOKED	ROACH	DOOBIE
BOWL	TOKE	BLUEDREAM
POUND	CANNABINOID	PURPLEHAZE

Word Search 3

```
V J B Q A H W D Y V P G J C W
O K I A C I D N I T I D L U Y
W T L H S I B A N N A C F S W
O W E H A L B H O H A R K J O
M G S V F S L D O P E U C H R
I Q E I Q I H K T R N B I S M
S C I Q F G B Q T K V I N Y W
P J D I R U R G C X U S O Q G
L L R F I M O S H L C C R T N
I F U T E J W I F S H O H B K
F P O A D D N S O V A T C J D
F U S R E V I K L L M T V V I
N C F E D K E Q Y N A I C G A
V J W R T G S Q Y M I M U O D
O B M M S E R W D P S S G G H
```

DOPE   SKUNK   SPLIFF
WEED   BISCOTTI   BROWNIES
CHRONIC   INDICA   FRIED
HASH   SOURDIESEL   CANNABIS

Word Search 4

```
D Y C A I T I I G H B O J T J
N E N M W N R L N G E Q F K Y
L K V V Q C B N T R G M Q G S
G M A R Y J A N E A M F P K J
U O T L H J F C I S B R A B N
N E F T W W V U A S A T M B T
K J H P A P E R S H V R N G N
F D F F S K A S P O R D E Y E
K E B Q R N L B E I J V S K Q
D Z N E G A H V S C C Y I E M
M T T C E D G F S K W N A N H
C I I B P H N W P O S R D S R
W L T O P S C Y S R Q J K C A
D B C G T F R E T H G I L K O
C H U Y T T A F H L F I A B U
```

EYEDROPS	BLITZED	FATTY
NUG	DANK	MARYJANE
POT	GRASS	AMNESIA
HEMP	LIGHTER	PAPERS

Word Search 5

```
C I S L D W I B S W I D G W V
I P D E V S D D J T O E F V S
H O V D T W A J N A G P Y G Y
G T D E K O M S C J H G E E S
I H H R A P J B M U S L W D T
J E L E U L W W C D A A Q F N
Q A L F E J K Y C T A D S E I
A D F Q J Z B T O N K D B N M
Q T B B H I M L Q Q T J U Y H
M M F T O R D Y H S I V V B S
W I Y W S W K K M H H Q U Y U
Y A D I S P E N S A R I E S K
H U Y A V I T A S S N I K S V
Y F I F J L G Y M R W U V U F
K I G F H C A O R V O G A Q W
```

GELATO   ROACH   PUFF
BUD   HYDRO   SMOKED
POTHEAD   SATIVA   GANJA
SKINS   DISPENSARIES KUSHMINTS

Maze 1

Maze 2

Maze 3

Maze 4

Maze 5

Maze 6

Maze 7

Maze 8

Maze 9

Maze 10

Sudoku 1

						9	3	
5	1	7	8				6	4
		9			6	8	7	1
	4	3				5		7
1		5	4			3	2	6
7		6		3			4	9
9		8		1			5	
			9	5	4	7	1	
	5			7	8	6		

Sudoku 2

		9	2				6	4
4		1			3			
8					6			
5	9	4	1	6	2	3		8
2			8	7	4	5		1
1			3			9	2	

(Grid continues with lower-left block joined)

1			3				4	8	6				3	7
5	4	9	6		8	7		3	4	8		6	5	9
2			9	4		6		5						2

		7					4	
	8	2	4	9	6		7	
	7				3			
7	1	4	8				3	9
	2	5						7
8		3	2	7	4	1	5	

27

Sudoku 3

Sudoku 4

Stoner Questions

(Even better when you play with a friend!)

1. Where was the first place you smoked and did you get high?

2. Favorite person to smoke with and why?

3. Indica or Sativa? Blunt, bong or brownie?

4. Favorite munchie food?

5. Smoking alone or with friends?

6. Favorite movie you've watched while high?

7. Weirdest place you've smoked?

8. Most amazing place you've smoked?

9. Any funny stories with your dealer?

10. Favorite smoke sesh' of all time?

Story Time

You've won the lottery and decided to adopt a bear, a tiger, and a monkey. What are their names and what adventures and activities do you plan on doing on with them?

_____
_____
_____
_____
_____
_____
_____
_____
_____
_____
_____
_____
_____
_____
_____
_____
_____
_____
_____
_____
_____
_____
_____
_____

Spot the Difference 1

33

Spot the Difference 2

Spot the Difference 3

35

Spot the Difference 4

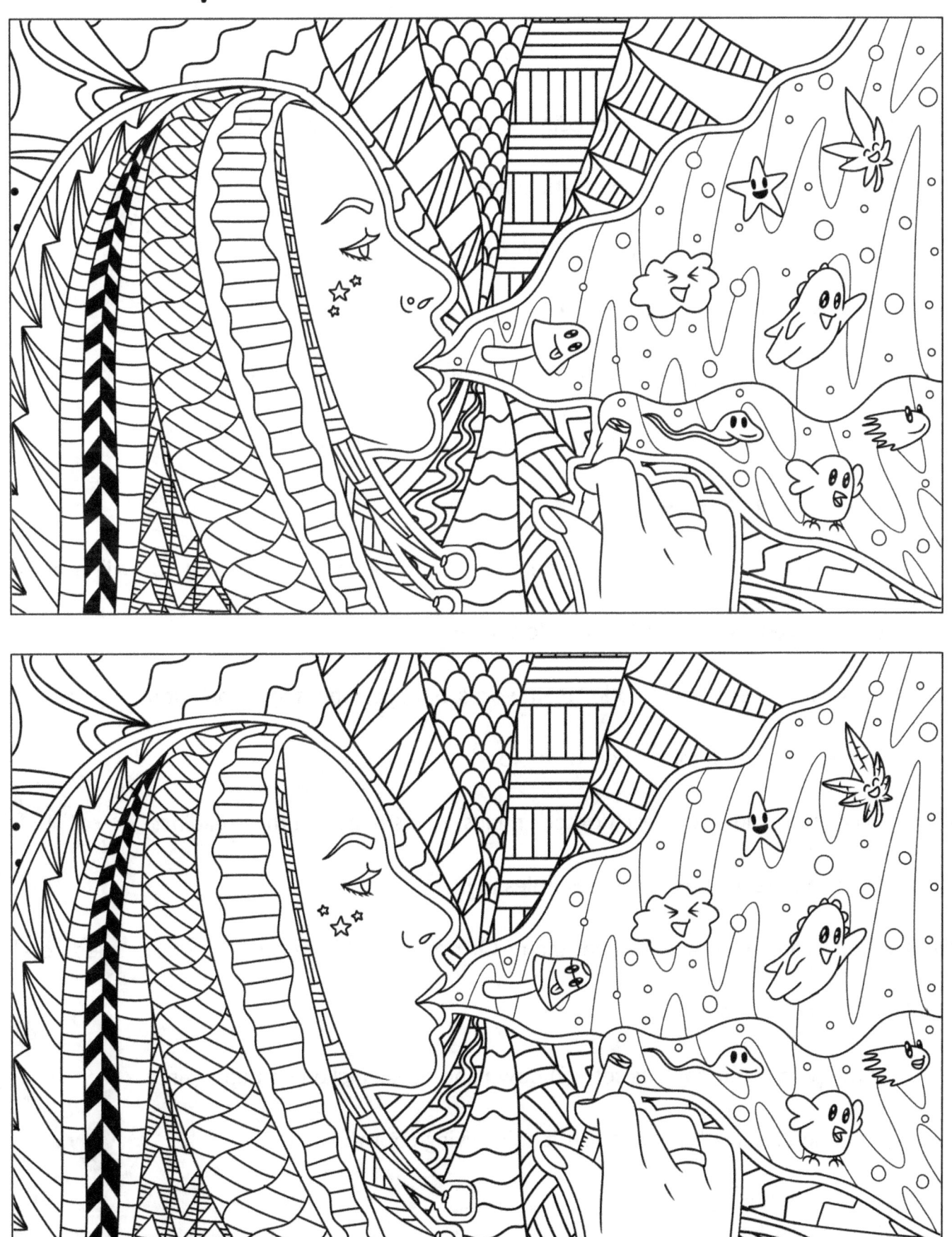

Stoner Thoughts

1) If you try to fail, but end up succeeding, which did you actually do?

2) Nothing is ever really on fire, but rather fire is on things.

3) How does a sponge hold water if it's full of holes?

4) If you smoke weed on a boat, does that make it seaweed?

5) If you drop soap on the floor, is the floor clean or is the soap dirty?

6) If you're in a competition by yourself, do you come in first or last?

7) What does water taste like?

8) Right now, you are both the oldest you have ever been and the youngest you will ever be again.

9) If you get scared half to death twice, do you die?

10) Actions supposedly speak louder than words, but speaking is also an action.

11) Ice cubes float in a pool of their own blood.

12) If two mind readers read each other's minds, who's mind are they reading?

13) If you rip a hole in a net it has less holes in it.

14) Are pets called pets cause we pet them? Or do we pet them cause they are called pets?

15) Which came first, the plant or the seed?

16) At some point, your parents set you down and never picked you up again.

17) If someone dies in a living room, is it still a living room?

Stoner Thoughts

18) If life is unfair to everyone, does that mean life is actually fair?

19) The word "bed" looks like a bed.

20) If you clean a vacuum, do you become the vacuum cleaner?

21) If you buy a bigger bed, you're left with more bed room but less bedroom.

22) Is it called the pilot episode because it's the first one they put on air?

23) Do you think the ocean is salty because the land never waves back?

24) Do you think sand is called sand because it's between the sea and land?

25) Technically, the brain named itself.

26) Is the "s" or "c" silent in scent?

27) An echo can't talk, but it can still reply.

28) If oranges are orange, why are limes not called "greens"?

29) Do pets name their owners?

30) Who decided the alphabet was in alphabetical order?

31) If tomatoes are a fruit, does that mean ketchup is a smoothie?

32) If you get out of the shower clean, how does your towel get dirty?

33) Being "up" for something means the same thing as being "down" for something.

34) Why do we get in a car but on a bus?

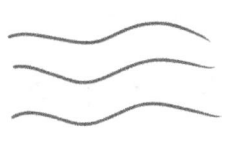

Joint vs. Spliff vs. Blunt

	Joint	Spliff	Blunt
Appearance			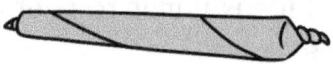
Contents	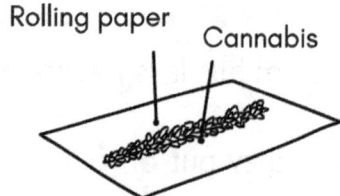 Rolling paper, Cannabis	Cannabis, Rolling paper, Tobacco	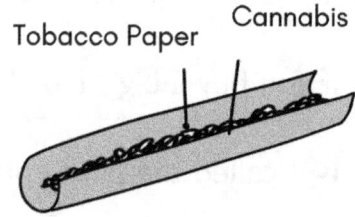 Tobacco Paper, Cannabis
Experience	Users experience the effect of cannabis only.	The effects of cannabis & tobacco are mixed, giving users a stimulating & energetic buzz.	Considered to be the heaviest hitter due to the interaction between the tobacco paper and the cannabis.
Quantity	Rolling papers are small, allowing for use if small quantity of cannabis.	Ratio of cannabis to tobacco can be easily varied.	 Tobacco paper is larger in size requiring larger quantity of cannabis.
Paper	Rolling papers are mostly made from hemp, flax, rice, or wood pulp. They can be plain or artificially flavored.	Rolling papers are mostly made from hemp, flax, rice, or wood pulp. They can be plain or artificially flavored.	Tobacco paper can be bought separately or obtained by hollowing out a cigar. Tobacco tends to have a sweeter flavor.
Burn	 Rolling paper burns more quickly	 Rolling paper burns more quickly	Tobacco paper is thick & burns slower
Popularity	More common in the United States & Canada	More common in Europe	Popular in communities

SATIVA

INDICA

Trees are taller & slimmer

Trees are shorter & bushier

Leaves are longer & thinner

Leaves are shorter & wider

- Head high
- Alertness
- Uplifting & euphoric
- Creativity
- Increased energy

- Body high
- Relaxation
- Appetite stimulator
- Sleep aid
- Pain relief

Best for day time use

Best for night time use

Medical use
- Fatigue
- Mood disorder
- A.D.D
- Appetite
- Depression

THC   CBD   THC   CBD

Medical use
- Anxiety
- Muscle spasm
- Insomnia
- Appetite
- Pain

Originated from
- Southern India
- Mexico
- Thailand

Originated from
- Northern India
- Afghanistan
- Malaysia

18 Ways to Get High

Best Movies to Watch Stoned

Ted
Superbad
Dodgeball
Bad Santa
Anchorman
Scary Movie
High School
Birds of Prey
Sausage Party
Grandma's Boy
The Big Lebowski
Pineapple Express
Dazed and Confused
Spider-Man: Into the Spiderverse
Harold & Kumar Go To White Castle

Mount Kushmore

1. Can you name these four legends?
2. Who would be your Mount Kushmore? Write down the four people you'd love to smoke with and why.

_____
_____
_____
_____
_____
_____
_____

Weed around the Globe

(Prices are in USD $ per gram)
Most expensive cities to buy marijuana:

1 Tokyo, Japan: 32.66
2. Seoul, South Korea: 31.07
3. Kyoto, Japan: 28.40
4. Hong Kong, China: 26.32
5. Bangkok, Thailand: 23.77

Least expensive cities to buy marijuana:

1. Quito, Ecuador: 1.29
2. Bogota, Colombia: 2.11
3. Asuncion, Paraguay: 2.12
4. Jakarta, Indonesia: 3.63
5. Panama City, Panama: 3.69

Highest weed consumption (metric tons)

1. New York, USA: 77
2. Karachi, Pakistan: 42
3. New Delhi, India: 38
4. Los Angeles, USA: 36
5. Cairo, Egypt: 33
6. Mumbai, India: 32
7. London, UK: 31

Lowest weed consumption (metric tons)

1. Singapore, Singapore: .02
2. Santo Domingo, Dominican Rep.: .16
3. Kyota, Japan: .24
4. Thessaloniki, Greece: .29
5. Luxembourg City, Luxembourg: .32
6. Panama City, Panama: .37
7. Reykjavic, Iceland: .44

Weed Brownies

For maximum bliss, take a week break to reduce your tolerance! Even a few days without smoking will significantly increase your high and enjoyment when that first brownie kicks in.

Calculating the bud
Hopefully you know what strain of weed you have, but if you don't, that's no big deal either. Just follow the numbers and start with a smaller serving when you eat it. You can always have more but you can't have less.

Get 6 grams of cannabis with 5% THC (you can usually do a quick Google search of your strain which will give you a rough % of how much THC is in it). This will be enough for 16 brownies.

Decarboxylating
Decarboxylation: the process that activates compounds in cannabis such as THC.

To get the most out of your bud you want to "decarb." Raw cannabis contains THCA which is nonreactive. When you smoke weed, it heats up to a certain temperature that loses a carbon dioxide molecule becoming THC. This is the part that has psychoactive benefits that smokers are after!

Usually simmering the cannabutter (cannabis + butter) doesn't convert all the THCA into THC. It can be done, (so you can do this if you're super lazy) but you'll be wasting a lot of it and you won't get the full effect.

To decarb, you want to put your 6 grams of weed, ground up into baking paper or aluminium foil, into your oven at 250 degrees Fahrenheit (120 degrees Celsius) for 30 minutes. This will prepare the bud making it psychoactive and ready to cook with.

Making the Cannabutter
1. Melt the butter on a low heat on a small to medium sized saucepan.
2. Add the decarbed bud to the melted butter and stir it every now and then.
3. Let it simmer on low heat for 45 minutes. It will begin to look like a dark green/yellowish color.
4. When the time's up, strain the butter using a metal strainer (tea diffusers work great) and use a spoon to press out all of the oil from the bud. Voila, you have your cannabutter!

If you really want to know how much of a difference decarbing makes, you can test the difference yourself. It's a simple test. Begin by eating a small nug and wait 60-90 mins. You'll get a little high but not as much as if you'd smoked that whole nugget. Now, grind another small nug and put it in some baking paper or foil and heat it to 250 degrees Fahrenheit (120 degrees Celsius) for 30 minutes. You're gonna be cooked! (P.S. Don't heat the weed at a higher temperature for less time, you might vaporize the good compounds like THC!)

Weed Brownies

Ingredients

- 125g unsalted butter, chopped
- 125g Cadbury baking dark chocolate, chopped
- 3 eggs, lightly whisked
- 335g (1 1/2 cups) white sugar
- 115g (3/4 cup) plain flour
- 30g (1/4 cup) Dutch cocoa powder
- 1 tsp vanilla extract
- Pinch of salt
- Cannabutter

Utensils

- 2 small bowls (for the chocolate & butter)
- 1 large bowl (to mix all the ingredients)
- Measuring cups
- Baking pan
- Mixing spoon
- Spatula
- Knife (to cut brownies)

1. Preheat oven to 355F/320F fan forced (180C/160C fan forced). Grease an 8 inch (20 cm base measurement) square cake pan and line with baking paper.
2. Melt chocolate on a stove top at low heat until it's all liquid.
3. Grease the baking pan.
4. In your mixing bowl, mix together the cannabutter, liquid chocolat, the brown sugar, and the vanilla extract
5. Beat the eggs.
6. Combine flour, cocoa, salt, and any optional dry spices in your second bowl.
7. A bit at a time, stir the dry mixture into the egg mixture until well blended. Do not overmix!
8. Spread the batter evenly into the baking pan, using the spatula or tablespoon to scrape all the batter out of the bowl.
9. Bake for 30 to 35 minutes, or until the brownie just barely begins to pull away from the edges of the pan. Another way to check is to stick a knife in. If it comes out clean, it's ready.
10. Finally, let it cool on a wire rack before cutting into squares, or if you're like me, pour the milk and dig in while they're hot!

Weed Facts

1) Who fully legalized cannabis first? As of 2013, Uruguay became the first country to fully legalize cannabis use. This includes consuming, selling, and cultivating plants. In 2014, Uruguay legalized cultivating up to 6 plants at home.

2) The word "canvas" is related to the word "cannabis." Historically, canvases were made of hemp.

3) Scientists have found that a marijuana compound can freeze and stop the spread of some types of aggressive cancer.

4) DMHP is a synthetic version of marijuana that was developed by the US military in 1949; the effects of the drug can last for days.

5) In college, Barack Obama was a member of the "Choom Gang," a group of boys who played basketball and smoked pot.

6) Since 2015, marijuana has become the fastest growing industry in the US. If marijuana becomes legal in all 50 states, the industry will become larger than the organic food market.

7) The first item sold over the Internet was a bag of marijuana over 40 years ago. Stanford students used Arapnet (an early form of the Internet) to buy weed from their counterparts at MIT.

8) "Bhang" is an Indian milkshake whose main ingredient is marijuana.

9) Marijuana is the most common illegal drug used in the United States. Approximately 100 million Americans have tried marijuana at least once, and more than 25 million have smoked it in the last year.

10) The name marijuana comes from a Mexican slang term for cannabis and is believed to have derived from the Spanish pronunciation of the names Mary and Jane (the two names were also common Mexican military slang for a prostitute or brothel.) Marijuana came into popularity as a name for cannabis in the US during the late 1800s.

Weed Facts

11) Cannabis seeds were used as a food source in China as early as 6000 BC.

12) There is a difference between hemp and pot. While hemp plants are the same species as marijuana plants, they don't produce the psychoactive ingredient (THC) that is in pot.

13) The first recorded use of marijuana as a medicinal drug occurred in 2737 BC by Chinese Emperor Shen Nung. The emperor documented the drug's effectiveness in treating the pains of rheumatism and gout.

14) The Rastafari religion considers marijuana to be one its sacraments.

15) Paraguay is believed to be the world's largest producer of marijuana.

16) Common terms for marijuana include reefer, pot, herb, ganja, grass, old man, Blanch, weed, sinsemilla, bhang, dagga, smoke, hash, tar, and oil.

17) Someone would have to smoke over 1,500 pounds (680 kilograms) of marijuana within about 15 minutes to die of a lethal overdose. In other words, dying from a weed overdose is nearly impossible.

18) Researchers discovered that chocolate produces some of the same reactions in the brain as marijuana.

19) Seattle, Washington, offers marijuana vending machines. Called ZaZZ, these machines take cash or coins, since the federal government doesn't allow people to buy marijuana with credit or debit cards.

20) The first two drafts of the United States Declaration of Independence were written on paper made from hemp.

Coloring Palette

There are two replicas of each coloring page, one with a regular background and one with an inverted black background. This way you can color your favorite pages twice or rip one out and color with your friend!

Test out your colors here before you get started to see which combinations go well together!

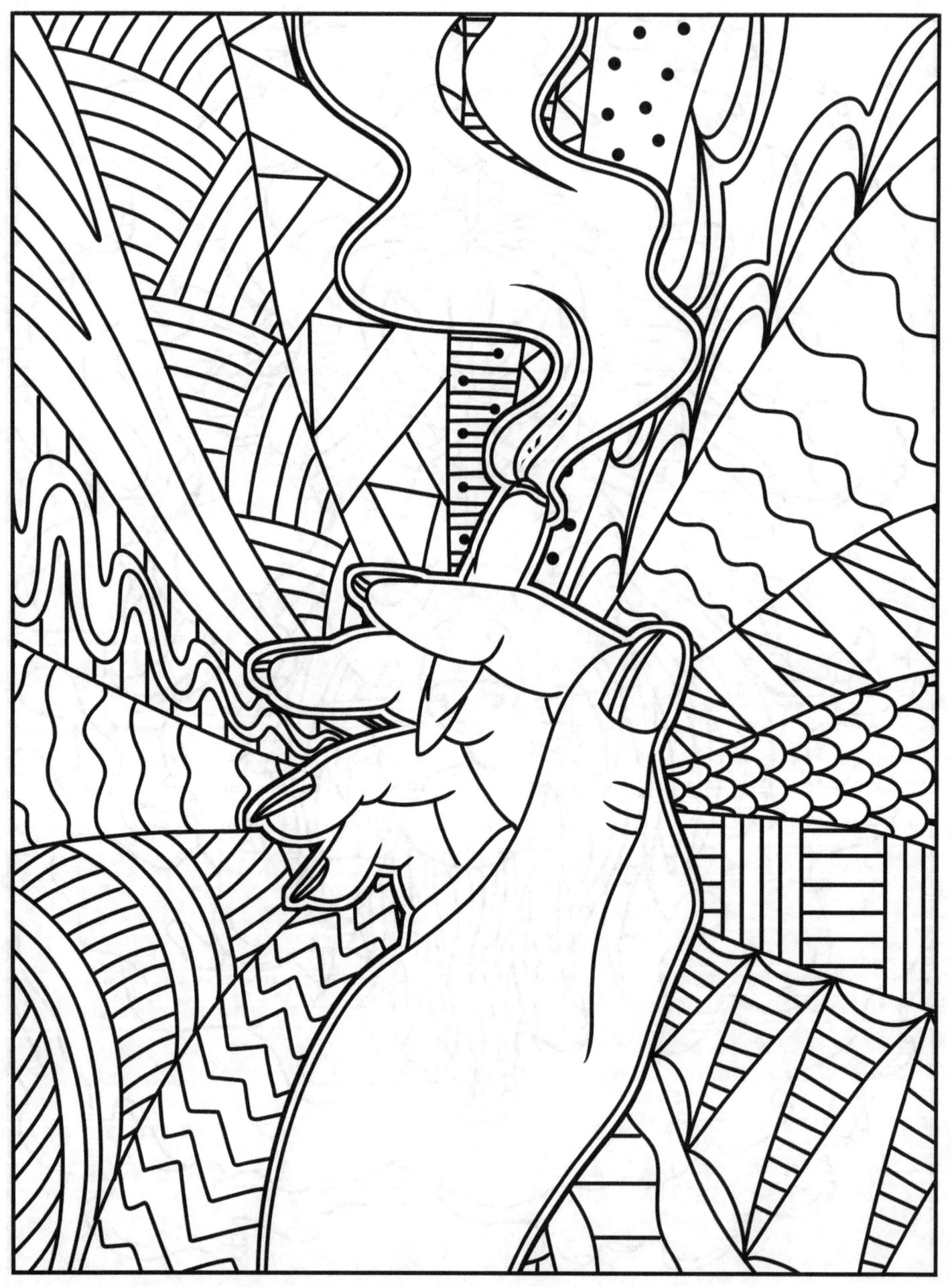

Answers 1

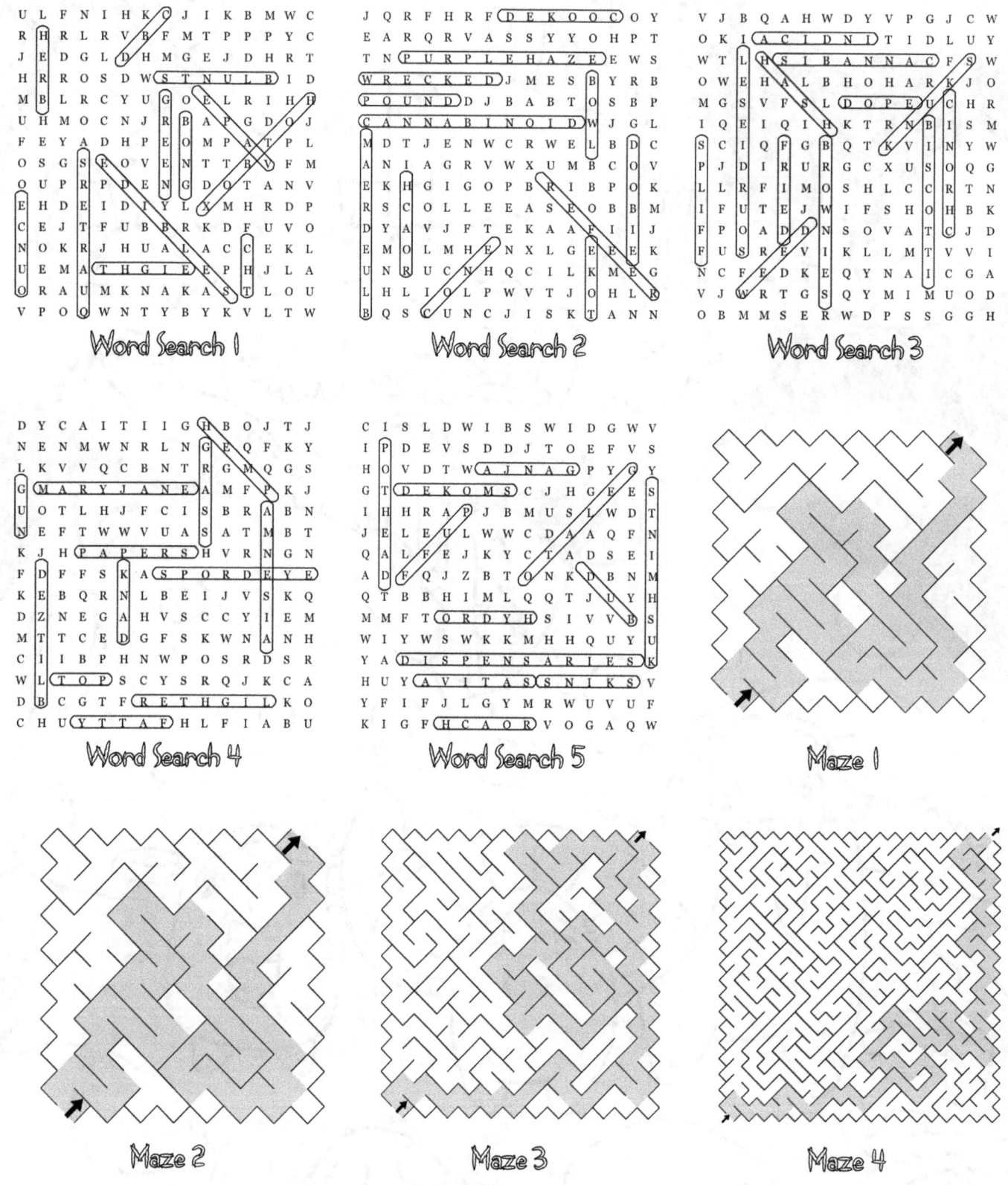

Answers 2

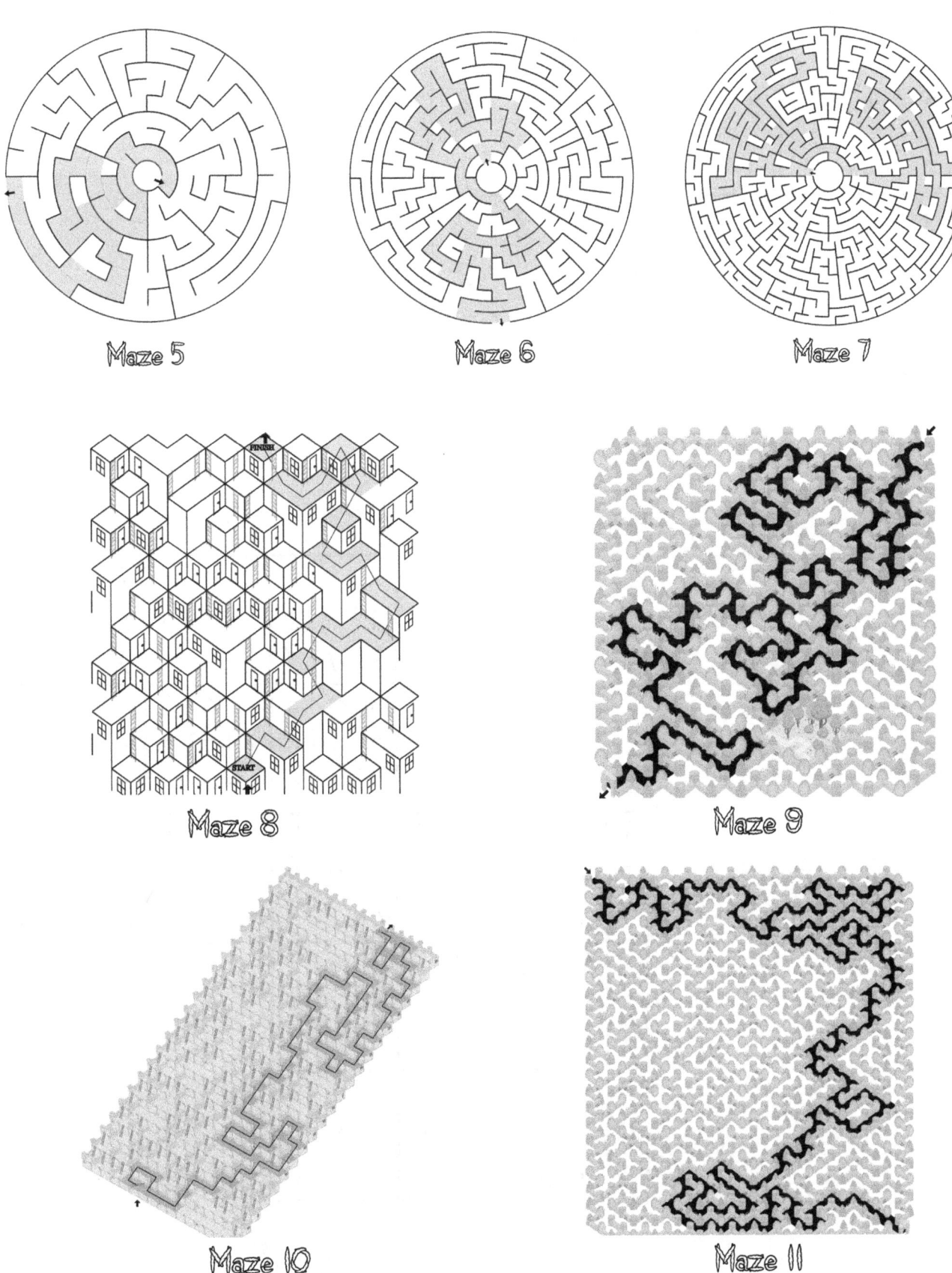

Maze 5

Maze 6

Maze 7

Maze 8

Maze 9

Maze 10

Maze 11

Answers 3

8	6	4	7	2	1	9	3	5
5	1	7	8	9	3	2	6	4
3	2	9	5	4	6	8	7	1
2	4	3	1	6	9	5	8	7
1	9	5	4	8	7	3	2	6
7	8	6	2	3	5	1	4	9
9	7	8	6	1	2	4	5	3
6	3	2	9	5	4	7	1	8
4	5	1	3	7	8	6	9	2

Sudoku 1

3	5	9	2	1	8	7	6	4
4	6	1	7	9	3	8	2	5
8	7	2	5	4	6	9	1	3
5	9	4	1	6	2	3	7	8
2	3	6	8	7	4	5	9	1
1	8	7	3	5	9	2	4	6
6	2	5	1	3	7	4	8	2
5	4	9	6	1	8	1	6	5	9
2	3	8	9	4	7	4	8	2

1	6	7	3	5	2	9	4	8
5	4	9	6	1	8	7	2	3
2	3	8	9	4	7	6	1	5
9	5	1	7	2	3	8	6	4
3	8	2	4	9	6	5	7	1
4	7	6	5	8	1	3	9	2
7	1	4	8	6	5	2	3	9
6	2	5	1	3	9	4	8	7
8	9	3	2	7	4	1	5	6

Sudoku 2

Answers 4

Sudoku 3

			4	1	6	7	8	3	9	5	2						
			7	9	8	5	2	4	6	3	1						
			5	3	2	9	6	1	7	4	8						
			8	7	4	6	1	2	3	9	5						
			1	2	9	4	3	5	8	7	6						
			6	5	3	8	9	7	1	2	4						
9	1	2	4	8	7	3	6	5	1	4	9	2	8	7	6	1	3	9	5	4
7	3	8	9	6	5	2	4	1	3	7	8	5	6	9	4	7	2	3	8	1
5	6	4	2	1	3	9	8	7	2	5	6	4	1	3	8	5	9	6	7	2
1	2	3	5	4	9	8	7	6				7	4	8	5	9	6	1	2	3
8	7	5	6	3	2	4	1	9				3	2	6	1	8	4	7	9	5
6	4	9	8	7	1	5	2	3				9	5	1	3	2	7	8	4	6
3	5	1	7	2	8	6	9	4				1	3	5	9	4	8	2	6	7
4	8	7	3	9	6	1	5	2				8	7	4	2	6	1	5	3	9
2	9	6	1	5	4	7	3	8				6	9	2	7	3	5	4	1	8

Sudoku 4

1	9	6	3	5	7	2	4	8				9	7	1	4	8	5	2	6	3
3	4	5	8	2	1	6	9	7				4	8	3	2	6	1	7	9	5
7	2	8	9	4	6	3	5	1				5	6	2	9	3	7	8	1	4
4	7	2	5	1	3	8	6	9				7	5	8	3	1	4	6	2	9
5	8	1	6	9	4	7	3	2				6	1	9	5	2	8	3	4	7
6	3	9	2	7	8	5	1	4				3	2	4	6	7	9	5	8	1
2	6	4	7	3	9	1	8	5	4	3	7	2	9	6	7	4	3	1	5	8
8	1	7	4	6	5	9	2	3	6	5	8	1	4	7	8	5	2	9	3	6
9	5	3	1	8	2	4	7	6	1	9	2	8	3	5	1	9	6	4	7	2
						3	6	2	8	1	5	4	7	9						
						8	9	4	2	7	3	6	5	1						
						5	1	7	9	6	4	3	2	8						
4	7	2	8	9	3	6	5	1	3	2	9	7	8	4	1	2	3	5	6	9
8	3	5	7	6	1	2	4	9	7	8	6	5	1	3	9	6	4	8	2	7
6	1	9	5	2	4	7	3	8	5	4	1	9	6	2	8	5	7	4	1	3
2	6	3	4	7	8	9	1	5				2	3	8	7	1	5	6	9	4
1	8	4	9	5	6	3	7	2				6	4	9	3	8	2	7	5	1
9	5	7	1	3	2	8	6	4				1	5	7	4	9	6	2	3	8
7	4	1	3	8	9	5	2	6				8	9	5	6	7	1	3	4	2
3	2	8	6	4	5	1	9	7				3	2	1	5	4	8	9	7	6
5	9	6	2	1	7	4	8	3				4	7	6	2	3	9	1	8	5

Answers 5
Spot the Difference 1

Spot the Difference 2

Answers 6
Spot the Difference 3

Spot the Difference 4

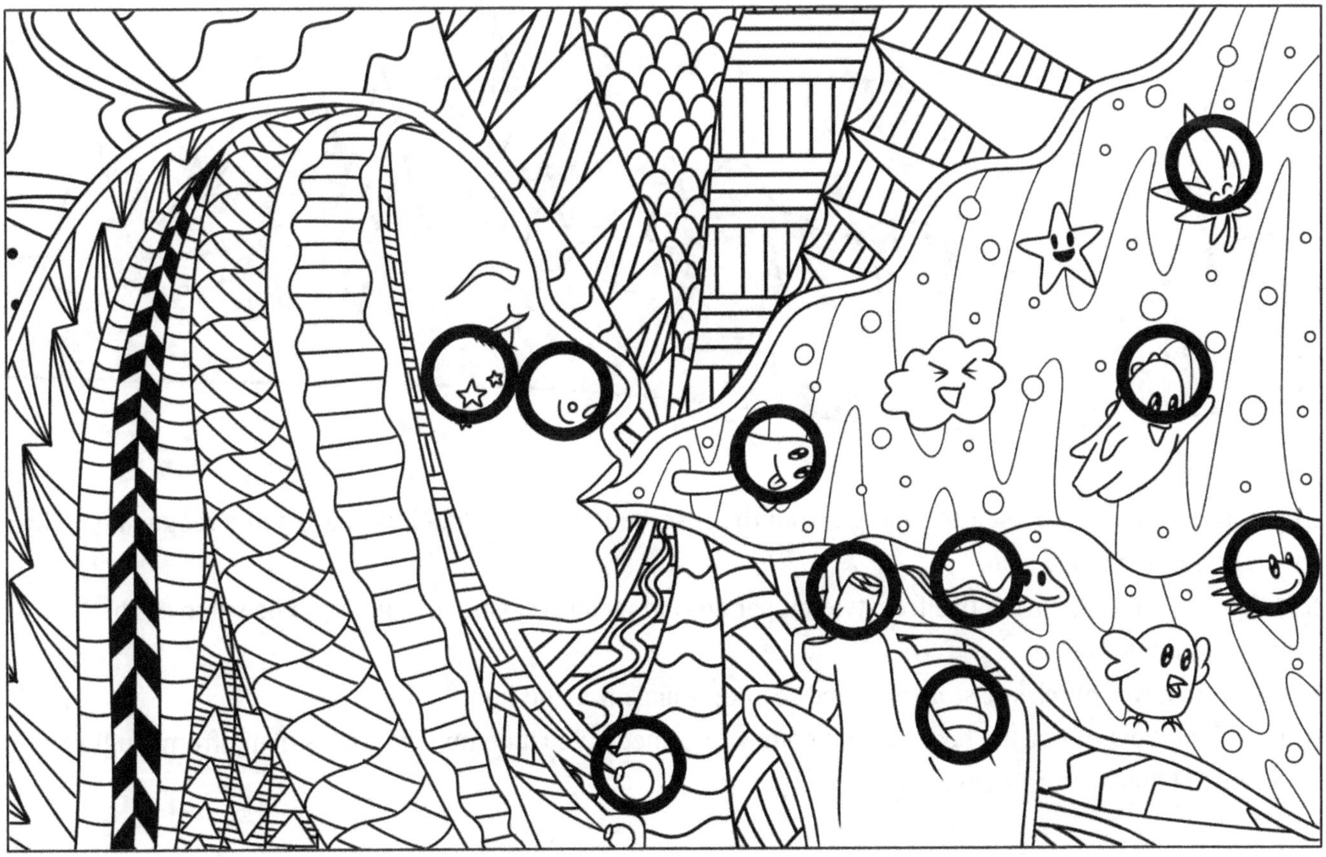

Mount Kushmore

1. Bob Marley
2. Snoop Dog
3. Seth Rogan
4. Dave Chapelle

1. First international superstar to emerge from the so-called Third World. Gotta have some reggae and why not with this famous pop icon.
2. With an IQ of 147, having this freestyle rapper around while you smoke is going to be some of the best entertainment around.
3. You gotta have this classic stoner around to keep things fun and light hearted.
4. One of the best, if not the best when it comes to comedy, you'll be on your knees dying from laughter after lighting a blunt with this guy.

Nora Says Thank You!

If you enjoyed the book, it would mean the world to me if you could leave a quick review on Amazon. It really helps out small publishers like me to get this book into the hands of others! You can do so by scanning the QR code below which will take you straight to the Amazon review page. Thank you so much in advance! ❤

P.S. If you'd like to see more of me and my content, be sure to follow me on Instagram! You can find me by searching @NoraReidColoring

www.ingramcontent.com/pod-product-compliance
Lightning Source LLC
Chambersburg PA
CBHW081354080526
44588CB00016B/2489